CAPTAIN COOK IN THE UNDERWORLD

ROBERT SULLIVAN

Captain Cook in the Underworld

AUCKLAND UNIVERSITY PRESS

An extract from this poem has appeared in *Chain* (US).

Auckland University Press
University of Auckland
Private Bag 92019
Auckland
New Zealand
http://www.auckland.ac.nz/aup

© Robert Sullivan, 2002

ISBN 1 86940 281 2

National Library of New Zealand Cataloguing-in-Publication Data
Sullivan, Robert, 1967-
Captain Cook in the underworld / Robert Sullivan.
ISBN 1-86940-281-2
1. Cook, James, 1728-1779—Journeys—Polynesia—Poetry.
2. Mythology—Poetry. 3. Songs, English—Texts. I. Title.
nz821.2—DC 21

Publication is assisted by

creative nz
ARTS COUNCIL OF NEW ZEALAND TOI AOTEAROA

This book is copyright. Apart from fair dealing for the purpose of
private study, research, criticism or review, as permitted under the
Copyright Act, no part may be reproduced by any process without
prior permission of the publisher.

Printed by Astra Print Ltd, Wellington

Alone, alone, all, all alone,
Alone on a wide wide sea!
And never a saint took pity on
My soul in agony.
     Samuel Taylor Coleridge,
      from *The Rime of the Ancient Mariner*

To get back up to the shining world from there
My guide and I went into that hidden tunnel;

And following its path, we took no care
To rest, but climbed: he first, then I – so far,
Through a round aperture I saw appear

Some of the beautiful things that Heaven bears,
Where we came forth, and once more saw the stars.
     Dante Alighieri,
      from *The Inferno* (translated by Robert Pinsky)

Because Rhyme remains the parentheses of palms
shielding a candle's tongue, it is the language's
desire to enclose the loved world in its arms;
     Derek Walcott, from *Omeros*

INTRODUCTORY NOTE

This poem was originally a libretto commissioned by the Orpheus Choir of Wellington to celebrate their fiftieth anniversary. The oratorio, *Orpheus in Rarohenga*, was composed by John Psathas, and at the time of writing will be performed in the Wellington Town Hall in November 2002 by the choir and the New Zealand Symphony Orchestra.

I dedicate this poem to my late grandfather, Massey Turi Sullivan.

Absolution Chorus

In this quadrant of the journey
we look to redeem from burning
James, a man of his day, in hellfire –
we have twenty-first century hindsight –

while he thought he discovered
these islands already discovered by lovers
Kupe and his wife Kuramarotini.
He didn't know to presume discovery

was a lie, nor did he know the prejudices
of the unborn colony. Forgive the Ulysses
of his day, for the mores of his age,
for overlooking the inhabitants with his claim.

We the choir absolve him. For this
is the absolution chorus. Forgiveness,
remember to forgive, hold
this as Cook and his story unfolds.

And now let us listen to James
stake out his claim for the greatness
of the angel Albion, her new dominion
over an innocent slip of land.

Summon the cast from the shades,
            hold a torch to their names:
bright Orpheus of the singing lyre,
            poet exemplar, inspired
by His Majesty's bark *Endeavour*: a choir

for *Endeavour* travelling to the transit of Venus,
            our Captain Cook's mission to see this:
Endeavour tossed about these deep waves,
            a coin landing lucky side for the brave,
Endeavour James! Endeavour James!

Loft the sails of our story; embark for a new start,
            an argosy in our Cook's heart:
Carl Jung more than a century in the future
            argues for the stories of ancient culture
lodestars for the psyche: here Orpheus

enters Cook's first voyage in fierce
            spirit, a bright star guiding Cook's choir.
Thus invisible Orpheus sings spirit songs of the lyre
            stoking passions for a distant fire,
for fiery Venus travelling across the heavens

Venus luring these Europeans
            for a glimpse of her in a glass,
to confirm an astronomical chart
            and the psyche's template
the starry temple of woman to our crewmates

and our musical stowaway: divine Orpheus.
            But enough talk from Jungian Olympus,
Orpheus and Eurydice, his heart's name,
            Orpheus' love in an underworld of flames.
Bring it back to Cook. Spyglass to the ready,

the Captain speaks, heading for Tahiti.
                    Ah Paradiso bliss!
These natives are the gentlest, a breezy caress
                while my crew
feast on all their senses can thrust and chew

from nativity. It's like Christmas!
                Christmas in the sun, and mistle-
toe on the stubbled chins of our lads
              from England. Even Joseph Banks
has let his hair down, great hats wear no hats at all,

these friendly islanders don't give a toss. Haul
              the anchor, first mate! and drop it again,
it's almost too much with Venus on the brain.
              Rule *Endeavour*! *Endeavour*
rules the waves, and soon the heavens!

Onwards for Venus! By King George
           it's hard to sleep on the voyage,
especially when every glittering light
           could be her skirting across the infinite night
taking my admiralty with her. Oh to sleep

without worries about sextants and angles, how deep
           this new bay, how friendly her inhabitants.
It's getting on my nerves I tell you. Oh for Morpheus
           and his retinue instead of all the fuss
for the crew. They're like babies: take your lime juice!

I'll whip every man who won't drink his juice!
           And still I have to whip them.
I'll whip any man caught with scurvy, take his rum,
           clap him in the hold
until he's better. Young and old,

[Endeavour crew*]*
The captain doesn't know his men,
we would follow him to the end,
out of the blazing native sun
sketched by Sydney Parkinson:
where Cook goes we go too!

But we don't just thrust and chew,
we're disciplined, we're English
through and through — Venus
is our mission, and exploration
next. We crew for the nation!

I'll whip them. I'm a fair captain by George,
    and I'll have my Whitby horde
free of scurvy. Look at the gracious
    natives. They aren't pretentious.
They're pleased with trinkets while we aim for Venus.

Starry goddess? Bah! We are enlightened
    men! To map heaven
and the dots beneath it. Beautiful dots I grant you,
    with flora fit for the new gardens at Kew,
but I say science first, that's the way, my motto –

find the passage! Make a sounding, on to
    discovery! I'll take one of their fry
back as a toy. HM will be pleased. Oh my Omai
    he'll say and make me Admiral Cook,
the big soft butterfly. What a great look.

And the greatest look is Venus. Tonight's
           the big night. We men of science
have calculated it. Spy scopes steady
           on the bridge, eyes ready
to stare. "But I say, Captain, she won't appear!"

"I say, James, I say." The crew say. "Where is Venus? I say,
           James." I say "Why do you assay
me?" I say "I am Captain Cook. And it is obvious
           where Venus is.
It is still there, and we are still here." (Each of us

must keep our heads.) I retire to the great cabin
           to tot. And what a tot. The habit
confuses me for once. I hear singing, unearthly
           music from a lyre. Forty feet
out to sea! A Greek claiming he's a deity,

Credence and Fort Venus [An Historical Note]

*Forgive the Orphic one his licence
even with science —
our orb did grace the cosmos of course....
the crew spied her from a fort*

singing like a bird, such beautiful words,
                how swiftly he picks his chords:
Your Venus in flames is no woman,
                she is no tender blossom
making her death an event.

Your Venus is an orb who does not cry you're absent.
                Your Venus is a pinprick in the sky
who doesn't understand the science of your sighs –
                do not deny your sadness, James.
Then go onwards, take your destiny and your fame . . .

Ship's master?! Fetch me the chart of the southern land
                and my compass – we have new plans . . .
hurry, lad. Hurry. What say you, Orpheus?
                I have retained your cautious
advice. Yes yes I know your name is Molyneaux.

A slip of the tongue. Oh my crew
            is so reliant on me – what do they think?
We believe in you, James, hold the tiller to the brink
            of Hades and beyond – we believe in you, James,
you're like a father to us. We were lost souls in the shade

until we crewed your ship. You're inspiring,
            it's like your sails are flying
through the cosmos of the ocean. Even Venus
            sings to you – bright Orpheus
plays the music while the goddess sings your name:

James. Do not fret my dear – I didn't appear in flames . . .
            there was a cloud. That's all. Fate
intervened against our meeting,
            but please listen to my singing,
for beauty and science intertwined in healing:

I am Venus, the morning star,
placed to guide you through the shades far
toward the southern land — the land of the cloud
that hides me now. Aotearoa of white alps
and deep harbours, a land you'll be proud

to call your own. I am Venus, the guiding light
and mistletoe of the ancients. I am the Aphrodite
of your spirit guide, the man of lyres and song —
Orpheus will do you no wrong on your long
argosy so go far, James and discover your south seas greatness.

Onward, James and remember me as a goddess
on your transit. Let this trip be the transit of night —
not the loss of a faint speck in the wilderness of sky . . .
go on, James and journey for the discovery
of great peoples . . . avoid the misery

*of ignorance and sermons, James. Look to history
for harmony – set out well as your acts precede you –
harmony, James, be harmonious with these people:
I am their star too. I know their mana,
their skill in crossing oceans – and your anger,*

*James, beware your anger – the Pacific peoples
are patient to a fault, they have followed me, like pilgrims,
across the heavens for thousands of years –
but remember you are the new ones here.
Take my warning to heart, and not to muskets: there!*

Hear the dreaming of the crew, our psyches in flight
while our bodies sleep – listen to the heavenly light,
Captain, listen, soul to soul we are your equals in heaven,
hear your dreaming crew as no miasma of the ocean.
We came far, from the lowest classes, with the chosen

men of the sciences – a social ladder
bent across the planet from Britannia.
Take heed, James, of singing Venus in flames.
Our Saxon ancestors knew the stars and fates.
Hear our blood calling you in a dream oh Captain.

Oh Captain don't be captured by mad men,
oh captain, our captain, oh our Captain look!
Ahoy, land ahoy, captain, land ahoy, Captain Cook!
Young Nick. Young Nick, what's the excitement?
Young Nick, what did you say? I am too frightened

to understand you – did you say land?
Aloud! land below those clouds!? Good lad!
Crew did you hear? Do you see that place?
Let's call it Young Nick's Head. By His Grace
I'll claim this all for His Majesty's domains!

Hurrah for Nick! A tot for every man aboard!
Drink up! Three cheers for Nick! What a call!
Discovery. Discovery again. We're crewing
for England and we're happy – at last great news,
no need to brood on Venus. Tomorrow we cruise,

row the boat ashore, hallelujah – there must be women
round those fires. Heaven-sent delirium –
maybe they have gold too? Nuggets
to pocket, and women to die for. How rugged,
oh ho how rugged exploration is!

We'll be famous! Making us most rugged of nations:
yo Britannia! Ho ho ho! Men settle down,
I want the cutter taken in for provisions, around
Young Nick's Head tomorrow. Good on you lad.
Draughtsman? We need to start a map,

*I want every detail of this place planned,
for as you know, this could be the Southern Land
of Ptolemy — the ancients knew their science
and now's the chance to prove our might!
To complete the chart of the planet — our purpose

to place Britain as the star of the world chorus:
a star shining on knowledge, a star shining
on kindness, a star shining on the crying
masses ignorant of the wisdom of the West:
our technical knowhow got us here, we're the best,

goodness knows how they did it. Who cares?
Sleep my good crew. Sleep. Tomorrow is forever
away when you step onto the southern land.
Sleep this night away. Sleep for England.
Go to Morpheus, gently into the night . . .*

Venus, I'm looking for you – in the waves at night.
              Venus out of sight
in black space. Oh mist and frigate birds,
                if only my hurt
from missing you wasn't for a star! Why turn?

Who am I missing? Is it my doom to wander
              a world alone? Why gather
stardust when I have my marriage to Elizabeth?
                Where is God's plan in heathenness?
I must sleep. God of the waves, I must lighten this.

We solemnly stake Great Britain's claim
          to sovereignty over this domain
which shall be known as New Zealand.
          God Save England
and the Hanovers! First we go round, then we go in –

we'll cut these islands from the ocean
          like a circumcision –
it's a snip on paper. Oh visions
          of arching mountains, aeolian breeze,
nubile and agile innocents dotted between the trees,

nay, pillars of wood fit for Athens! A land
          for gods like the Greeks and Romans,
these innocents belong to this paradise lost
          for all time until now, our ship-tossed
crew has rediscovered their lust for life,

and their unfortunate hosts. Another template lies
              in the Western story of these islands,
well insular, well bedded, the Cook model,
              the statues – pillars turned to rubble
in postmodern society. But back then they were wow!

Muskets blatting like ghetto blasters, pow!
              They were the imperial cool,
the vanguard of the coolest king to rule,
              from the far side of another ocean,
flag-fluttering history set in motion.

Bang! They all fall down!
              Bang! Britain's the talk in town,
let's make Cook a deity. Hail Da King!
              The biggest kill machine
with a crew to match – just look at that hat,

he's gotta be a god, blat blat blat!
                        We the peoples of this island
assure you, Cook God, we are frightened
                        and beg you to stop killing
our people. Your men find it thrilling

to kill us – so it's anything you want
                        great powerful Cook, but don't
kill us anymore. We aren't gods. We bleed
                        when you whip us, we scream
at your fire sticks – and we die

from the illnesses of gods. Give us time
                        good Cook, to learn. We are humbled
by your divine kindness in seeking us, but
                        dear divine holiness please care,
see our wretched confusion and spare

your needy servants pain.
                What what? First mate
can't understand a bloody word – another volley
                to stop their sorry
prattle. Tell them to send more food –

fine-looking natives though. A new
            sketch, Joseph, the physiques
of these natives will fetch a pretty penny
            from the quaffers of Whitehall
for my next expedition, ho ho, hide the musket balls –

come come young gent – sketch!
            The poor fey wretch.
A handkerchief won't hide the blood,
            not like a good dusk
dabbed in the background – there!

Oh the Admiralty's orders? They were clear,
           'tis sad, but the shooting, 'twas defence
of the true king's men
           against barbarity, fine barbars
granted, but nevertheless far from equals – ah, ah

it is a shame. I must retire to good Solander's library –
           all the classics, timely homilies
dredged from antiquity. What's this one? Orpheus.
           My friend of the vision. Oh hideous
fortune – my only friend a shadow.

And so onwards and onwards I go,
           following the admirals in a blur
of Endeavour, Discovery, Resolution, astir
           in the Pacific pond I made
for England. My journeys are parades

painting the world map pink.
                But what to think?
The admirals will send me on forever,
                waving on their flag-bearer,
past the Pillars of Hercules where flags mean

nothing! I can shoot natives clean
                through and they die
amazed at our power, no anger, or fright,
                they just *die*.
It's disquieting to follow.

These same natives make me a hollow
                tree, an idol, praise me as divine Lono,
dress a temple in white feathers
                give me fine head-dresses
and then rob me, dazzled by their flattery!

Bottles, nails, cups, plates, clothing, ropes, cutlery,
                out they go, guzzled in the villages –
what did we do to deserve this? We are adventurers
                calling in for r and r,
but this place treats us as a free-for-all bazaar . . .

by crikey, I'll show them who's boss, a crackdown,
                let's toss some gunpowder around –
load balls not shot, I want bodies on the beaches,
                just like in New Zealand –
nine dead in the first couple of days, a sad affray,

they challenged us and we responded, again
                and again we wandered the coasts
they'd meet us in their dugouts, most
                were hostile – it was easier for them
to die from ball than bear the scars from shot – condemn

me, I dare you, but these natives were scary,
    they gave no quarter, were daring
in the way they fell – weren't easily scattered
    by cannon, not that it mattered
to the bloody business of death – wanted to trade

straight away . . . so this business to Hawaii's shame
    should be settled divinely,
they stole the god Lono's boat, then I say finally,
    retribution is mine! Nothing's grander,
I should confer with the gentle Solander

of the library, his botanical perspective,
    and his judgement will be corrective
to a balance I fear is lacking within me –
    I keep hearing that entreating
lyre, the Orpheus chap, above the slap

and heave of waves. Like Venus that grabs
                my heart, so Orpheus crabs
my brain, sends it scuttling for a gull to swallow,
                tricks as old as the father of Lono,
following time gone troppo,

hairy waves rolling below *Endeavour*.
                And how these people adore
me as a God. They have made a temple
                to *me*, Lono-Cook, a pimple
on the deities of Solander – a common wooden

idol. How the Mother Church would spit
                on me if they knew me as an idol,
a poor sinner following a Polynesian festival
                circling an island like Hades –
is this the life of an immortal? To feast on shades,

sip the beauties of the Pacific offered
             in my honour? What
of the children these women will beget me?
               Will they be gods? Or social freaks
offered for heathen sacrifice? Is this a book

or the journey of a mind that was Cook's?
               Look! I see him now,
man stirring waves and heavens at the prow –
               set this Whitby Cat for departure, men!
We must be off, away from this sirens' den,

lead the way, good Orpheus, lead our argosy
               our leprous cargo of VD
stashed with lower and higher men, quills
               spilling ink, guns for the kill,
so many bodies, bodies set me to chill,

so Banks and Solander were disturbed . . .
                    I was too I swear – I have turned
my blankets black with the blood of these almost men,
           felt near to their women, aye, *cared*
for them as we caressed – felt my heart wrench,

I . . . I prayed for their souls as they bled,
                it stirred my heart to see them die – Banks
will testify. I hate quick deaths, can't stomach that
             mismatch, savages versus
the fire of marines. What did they have? Curses!

War dances! Wild features, ferocity.
              Even as we fired their nobility
shone through – as good as us in battle, no doubt,
             but we couldn't lose out,
we had *people* on board, mercy was too risky,

no we had to shoot. We started with small shot,
                but soon I had them load the lot
with ball – the savages were too brave, shoot to kill
                was the order, there was no thrill,
just the slow dance of men bleeding to death –

they advanced until their tonges hung not in threat,
                they were dead. Where their spirits
go who knows? I still prayed for these men at night,
                I could have slept with their wives –
you know what comes around goes around . . .

and now I issue a new command, we are tired out,
                so to speak, wink wink, a new
spell at sea would refresh the crew,
                they'd get their sleep –
so sail, good ship, sail . . . out into Davy Jones's keep –

beyond the reef, move it lads, faster, it's in my bones,
            we have to leave. Bring my telescope –
I want the widest part of the horizon, away
            from Canada, away from shades –
these ghosts of natives haunt me. I'm not God!

I'm not God! I'm not Lono either. My God
            lives in London, and will grind
my bones at idolatory. It opened my eyes,
            to be divine, but back to the ocean,
back to a world of brick and mortar, my broken

vows – as a god I had wives but no wife. This is wrong,
            a man needs a wife, just one to long for,
for now my longing is three times stronger
            than when I left Whitby. Steer
the Cat by the coast, a storm rolls,

and we must clear our heads of its noise –
                turn her round, back to the bay, hoist
the halyards, let them know we're back!
                Our mainspar has cracked, Captain –
when we anchor we'll get some timber – it'll be a while,

and I daresay our gluttony last time left some bile
                ashore – tell the men to be wary,
no comfort women, no stealing, nothing scary.
                We're going to be model English neighbours!
We'll triumph over our inclinations!

But alas I speed through my journal to my fate.
                Not a week has passed and they
have stolen our long-boat! – these Hawaiians
                must pay in blood. That's mine –
I'll have my boat back. They're asking for a scare!

Send marines with balls in their muskets. Strike fear –
                shoot once in the air.
Then shoot to kill, may God save these natives' souls
                for their bodies will be full of holes –
if these idolaters have souls, indeed if I have one –

does the god Lono have a soul? What far-flung
                destiny awaits me, far from the altars
of my Whitby youth? There are no stars
                to steer this course, for heaven
has turned me on the compass needle heading

nowhere. The marines are nearly ashore. I raise
              my arm, cock the pistol, aim,
and shudder from the report, and then I myself
              am felled – I'm felled –
I am lying face down in the water . . . bleeding

the sea red around me . . . I am part of the sea!

The sea closes around Cook like a mother,
              takes him in as another
drop in the ocean, speck in the sea,
              a bit of flotsam floating free
in the wreck of a dissolving dream . . .

Out of body, out of breath, Cook joins Orpheus
              at the lyre – his friend's chorus
a song to torch the watery pyre
              that is Cook's fate, that gyres
up a spout to take our great Cook's soul

down into the great sea. And so goes the old
            him: *I sing to Zeus as always,*
and the pantheon of my brother heroes, always,
            but now I take off that cloak of culture
and wear the culture of the Pacific, your soul's future,

dear Cook. I sing in my Maui throat,
            lying in wait with my brothers to slow
the sun of heaven, diving far out from Reinga,
            into the Underworld, Rarohenga,
and like Maui, you too have been wreathed in red

by the goddess of death. James, you are dead.
            But yet you have the chance to know
what you have done in life. Not for show. You are at the lip
            of the vortex of death. Slip
and your soul, your integrity, will be thrown

in your face – your soul too will be
                remembered for the shootings.
I offer you another journey, Captain.
                Take this challenge.
I don't offer you redemption, just integrity by chance.

Shootings? Well Sir Joseph was uncomfortable
                and I wasn't doing it for the fun.
I had a ship to protect, an expedition, I needed
                to set boundaries, to be expedient
for the sake of the mission. They were natives!

Good captain, I am not here to grade this.
                There are no jurists
in the cosmos of the sea – just wanderers,
                don't you wonder, explorer
that you were, about the souls you sent

to wander here? The vast descent into death
                that you begat? For your soul
to rest, good captain, you must meet them, soul
                to soul, until the earth in mercy
enfolds you – until then you're nursing

a zombie soul forever searching for its tomb.
                Confront your doom
and follow me on your last argosy –
                into Rarohenga, gross Hades,
deep into the underworld of souls,

a land of idols not Eldorado gold.
                Come Cook, Lono, harrier,
meet the souls brought here by warriors,
                and by your unequal muskets –
if your soul is to cease wandering, then face justice,

the dead brought here at the hands of your men.
            For these were men, people, humans
scattered like seeds in killing fields.
            Captain, you have sown these.
Now eat your fill, the souls of your discovered lands . . .

Let's start furthest south, in New Zealand,
            the deepest shades of Hades,
truly an underworld of icy craters –
            a wonderland of people, orators
and warriors, artists and singers,

laughers and priests. People of conduct.
            People with flaws including trust,
but now, Captain, you have a chance to explain,
            to take away the pain
that your descendants will bear,

to show that England cares!
               Tell them, Captain! Tell them
you care! *"Good Orpheus, I cannot share*
               my reasoning with shadows,
make these silent ones come out – invoke

their humanity and not their disdain.
               I want to see them see my shame –
it is my shame. My shame at killing innocents,
               my shame and not my descendants'.
Let me see their features, the fine chiselled faces

of their leaders. You talk of people. Let me make
               my statement in the light.
Let me see them in the day, and understand their plight.
               Good Māui who stalled
the racing sun of heaven. Call them to talk,

to begin to talk." Very well, Cook, for you I haul
              the sun again – now look at those natives!
Begin your speech and remember this isn't an oblation.
           Good people, men of this nation,
I ask you to hear me. We brought you aboard

as curiosities, as traders, a source
           of food and trinkets
and you treated us well. All I offer is this –
           we had to protect this ship.
Men of the highest ranks of the British

were members of our crew. Scientists
           brought ten thousand miles
to study you. We meant no harm, our style
           brought no incidents –
just a few warning shots, a little discipline

for the greater good. Our expedition
              would take the Maori to the world!
To risk us would be to risk your heralds!
              We discharged our mission
so well we were returned anon

on the third trip – hurled into the cannon
              by the greed of admirals
exploring good news, an adorable
              distraction from America. What's past
is past but yes I tired, lost my temper, blasted

broadsides instead of talking. We knew that
              you were human,
our kind, but so uncivilised we believed
              you were a grade below us.
And so this is my position. We were agents

of a greater power, and determined to maintain
                our height – for death is a leveller.
Witness my forced evidence here,
                in this cold hell . . . ." Thank you, Captain.
Thank you for acknowledging that

these people were people, face to face.
                I now ask that you turn to face
my only witness, the soul of a chief
                of the coastal middle east
of the North Island. A leader who dared

to stare your barrels down. He will share
                his story nameless.
Not to enflame you, nor to leave you blameless.
                He will not upset
the unending line of his descendants

stretching through the respected
                land, Aotearoa. E Kara,
tēnei te mihi atu ki a koe, te rangatira.
                    Timata tō kōrero pouri.
Mauria te wairua o te whenua kauri.

I turn to you, Kuki, a dead man to a revered one.
                I talk to you and cannot
make light of your devastation. My people
              suffered your diseases.
My people, mutilated, murdered, by your wormy crew.

If I could resurrect you Kuki I would I'd . . . I hate you
              with the passion of the dead,
with the passion of those bones piled on my head.
              I am glad you are a groaning
nightmare soul flying like a gull of the ocean.

[Orpheus:] Death is a shallow sea Kuki.
            You'll hit land. You see,
they have eternity to forget.
            You are safe from specks
in eternity. History is writ small in eternity.

You're a ghost, a roaming soul, Captain without mercy.
            They built you statues, named
a nation after you! Your reputation
            is like a navigator's
star. Cook, you are forever.

Why inflict this visit on me – the pain,
oh I am sorry, I would be your friend
in another world, I make this claim
from remorse – oh to see the dead
I made dead. Oh Lord how I cry!

You're one of England's finest.
                        But have you learned?
Have you learned? Have you learned
                        what you have to learn?
This is no dream Cook. You must learn

so that your soul will stops its journeying.
                        Cook! Stop your turning,
face me and tell me what you've learned.
                        "Learned? I have yearned
for Venus, my heart burnt in hellish desire –

now I am sent into a land of fire,
                        Hades, Rarohenga, sails
aflame in a dead ocean – the gods here
                        are foreign, I can't bear
the pain – my crew gone into the shades

with only a character from Solander's pages –
                you, a cartoon, to guide me,
navigator of the Pacific! Learned? That the sea
                rises and falls? I have craved
a thousand times my admiral's hat,

followed my letters faithfully, that
                is the only lesson to learn –
to serve one's masters, to earn
                one's keep. How can I profess a strange
god knowing I was equally strange?

Remember? 'Twas Lono they chanted,
                the true god of my heart
purged in a thatched temple to me. Agh!
                I learn nothing.
Not a thing.

But I will amuse you, Māui of the page,
*　　　　　　I will dissolve this stage*
and listen. I will listen to the ocean.
*　　　　　　I will turn to my emotions –*
take a spirit's leap from the cape

into the sky – I see him now, the crying skyfather,
*　　　　　　and look down harder*
into the face of the earthmother. Oh tears
*　　　　　　are easier now. The years*
do dissolve me. These tears reveal

more than a lachrymose mapmaker –
*　　　　　　I see the ridges, the moko and craters*
on the face of the great leviathan, Aotearoa,
*　　　　　　we are all callers*
faced with the noise of the surf . . .

the red surf of my once red blood,
                  the surf of an emotional flood –
how I looked and looked for Venus!
                  Ah I understand, Orpheus.
I understand, Māui, in my head, in my heart –

these souls of the shade, these destinies taken
                  by my shots and my blades,
these fine family men, these carvers and hunters,
                  these wearers of fine cloaks, no blunter
orators, singers of the finest poems of their land –

I understand. Now Māui I understand.
                  Sir Joseph Banks was disgusted
at the sight of the killing of such men
                  and now I understand him.

I truly understand. But my speech is late,
               too late for an explorer of fate,
too late to explore the heart, the soul of the matter,
               too late to sew up scores
of bicentennial corpses . . .

too late to revisit, unpick, revise
               our deeds . . . bandage and patch eyes,
poultice infections, scrape off the sores
               from privates we took as whores . . .
I say this as a soul with little effect on history,

the life I lived has been lived, its little necessities
               played out in ditties of a soul
like wind out of a clay-stopped hole.
               Now let me die, send this spirit out
to Hawaiki, send me out knowing this, send me now. . . .

So now, I, Orpheus and Māui, place your breath
on the bough of the tree clinging to the breast
of Reinga . . . your breath, your sigh, I throw these petals
to the temple of souls. Red. Reddest petals.
Their veins colour and break, spilling, taking heart.

And while your spirit flies its last,
take a look back on an explorer's past,
weigh those other souls against your own
and cease to wonder. Please know this thing.
Know this Cook. Know anything!

And now I pluck a line of poets turned in unison
                                                                 to the sun
following the warmth of unseen rays until they splay
on vowels with colours. Homer Curnow Dante
Rimbaud Tuwhare Baxter – Māui and Orphic blood.

ACKNOWLEDGEMENTS

My thanks go to Kuʻualoha Hoʻomanawanui at the University of Hawaiʻi, Mānoa for communication about the Makahiki Festival, Cook and Lono. Special thanks to the English Department at UH Mānoa for giving me the time and income to complete this poem while I was the visiting writer. In particular I thank Professors Caroline Sinavaiana, Rodney Morales, Susan Schulz and Paul Lyons for their hospitality, and my creative writing students for their inspiration.

WORKS CONSULTED

Beaglehole, J. C. *The Life of Captain James Cook*. (London: Black, 1974)
Graves, Robert. *Greek Myths*. (Harmondsworth: Penguin, 1955)
Obeyesekere, Gananath. *The Apotheosis of Captain Cook: European Myth-making in the Pacific*. (Princeton: Princeton University Press, 1997)
Robson, John. *Captain Cook's World: Maps of the Life and Voyages of James Cook R.N.* (Auckland: Random House, 2000)
Sahlins, Marshall. *How "Natives" Think: About Captain Cook, For Example*. (Chicago: University of Chicago Press, 1995)
Salmond, Anne. *Two Worlds*. (Auckland: Viking, 1993)